words gone wild

words gone wild

poems by

d. ellis phelps

Cover design by Shay Culligan

Cover art by d. ellis phelps

ISBN: 978-1-954353-92-3

Kelsay Books
502 South 1040 East, A-119
American Fork, Utah, 84003

for my grandchildren: Logan, Brady, Jack & Lily

Acknowledgments

Bulverde Standard (1988): "at seven"

Contents

the longest shadow

down the garden path

at seven

yellow cradle rocks to school
in the morning crisp and cool

little children scream and shout
lights a flashing say *watch out*

mother standing   waves goodbye
wipes a little tear from eye

hands in water starts to pray
keep my babies safe all day

mother's song

these are the hands that crumble the bread
hands that make sure the family is fed

hands that launder stinky clothes
hands that wipe the baby's nose

hands that lead the long   long way
hands that work while children play

hands that answer midnight calls
hands that comfort children's falls

hands that unknot knotted hair
—catch a fly ball in the air

hands of tents and tree house climbs
hands of dolls dressed up to dine

hands that build the garden wall
hands that help a child grow tall

after bath with stories read
hands that snuggle into bed

folded hands—prayers said
hands that hold small sleepy heads

careful hands   so soft and strong
—hands that sing a mother's song

morning sky

hunting cat crouching low
under gray germander goes

deftly hides deadly claws
inside sharpened feline paws

calico haunches primly sit
pounce to capture sparrow flit

feathered prey flees from spy
makes escape to morning sky

morning meal

unsuspecting honey bee
flying by the cedar tree

landed in the spider's web

though the insect tried to flee
smart arachnid—quietly she

down to capture quickly sped

grabbing victim by the head
spitting web and spinning legs

deftly wrapped her tangled prey

satisfied that she'd be fed
—making certain he was dead

spider carried honey bee away

tidy spider

threading thin black needle legs
with white warp and waft—
zippity zigged
zippity zagged
—a focused weaver at her craft

round as a quarter striped black and yellow
quick and clever her web she made
zippity hooked zippity hung
her silky trap was laid

all summer we lounged by the cool blue pool
my garden companion and i
zippity sat
zippity waited
for bloody mosquitoes buzzing by

through steam and storm on her web she stayed
patient   steadfast—so no surprise
zippity grabbed
zippity stuffed
and that fat spider grew twice her size

red leaves fall from naked trees
nothing is left where she and her web were
zippity packed
zippity split
now that's what i call a tidy spider

ladybug

lovely lady lunching on the dandelion leaf tiny
orange   winged creature   spotted black beast

doing business   making gossip   runs up and down
ladybug living in a dandelion town

bug hug

it's a very long walk
      for a caterpillar dad
from the bare spot in the grass
      to his den

do you think that when he gets there
      he'll recline in his big chair

do you think he'll need a hug
      when he gets in

beetle beat

big black beetle
scurries cross the street

where can he be going
in this horrid heat

perhaps he goes to beetle-land
to find another beetle and

with slightest wave of beetle hand
invite her out to eat

amphibian feast

back porch frog—sitting still
like a rock under windowsill

patient frog   big-eyed stare
—yummy bugs in summer air

clever frog   lightning tongue
croaking throat—nighttime song

hungry frog   getting thinner
waits to catch mosquito dinner

under the moon

lying here scratching on this old black cat
i can't think of anything finer than that

under the moon   lying right down flat
him on my tummy   me on my back

kadydid singing in the dark elm tree
—catfully relaxing

my cat & me

haiku

wrens   chatter and warn
cat hunts at the cyclone fence
wild petunias bloom

map of the world

oak limbs wind the sky
leaves lick the thirsty air

each coil going awry
first this way   then that

like the evening flight
of the midsummer bat

dip and swirl   turn and toss

impulse
reach
gnarl
curl

—wooden lines on the map
   of the world

skipping

down the garden path
a butterfly i spied

i thought to run and
get my net

instead

i let her fly

mud pie

a little time

hot diggity hot   hop hippity hop
take a shiny penny to the candy shop

tip toe tee   see what you can see
pick a piece of candy   count one two three

pop it in your mouth   shaky shaky shout
suck air in   blow a bubble out

not too big—stop
don't let the bubble pop

oh! wait—it's too late
now there's gum all over your face

gum in your hair   gum everywhere
you have to get that out of there

go to wash it in the kitchen sink
but the fat cat's sipping himself a drink

meow said he   *yeow* said she
try as you might you can't get free

call for help   screcch and yelp
down flies the parrot from the kitchen shelf

oh! my tithers   now you're covered in feathers
meow wear and kid's hair all stuck together

here comes mama now   *oh! no! don't tell me how*
all mama heard was a pitiful meow

well she said *this will not do*
and by the time mama got through

parrot   cat and bubble girl
were missing every single curl

she left no hair   no fur no feather
she sat those three all down together

she said *now don't you worry dears*
there's no reason for any tears

because mama knows when things go wrong
it won't take too very long
for everything to be just fine
if you will give it a little time

sloppy sister kisses

my brother says that snakes are cool
—he says they live in our swimming pool

that is not true!   i told him so
i said he really had to go   *just go*

i said it in my biggest voice
—and that he simply had no choice

but he would not go and then he said
bugs can crawl inside your head

that is not true!   i told him so
i said he really had to go   *just go*

but he would not go and then he said
late at night when you're in bed
a creepy giant   mean and red

comes sneaking in   i've seen his eyes

stop! i said *these are all lies!*

but he would not stop so I had to do it
i held my breath to help mc through it

i kissed him on his freckled nose
i kissed him on his stinky toes

i kissed his neck and back and pits
i kissed 'til he was kissing sick

he's the one who pleaded then
he screamed and squealed and shouted *when!*

so now   instead of all this fuss
we've shaken hands the two of us

he'll keep his lies and bugs and hisses
i'll keep my sloppy sister kisses

lily hyacinth winifred pearl

—after shel silverstein

lily hyacinth winifred pearl
is a very   very pretty girl

she can dance and sing and tap
she can set a booby-trap

lily pearl is quite quite able
to set a place at a fancy table

she can write a book
draw and cook

sew and knit
or daintily sit

she can jump a rope
bait a hook

throw a ball
but   that's not all

no. that's not all!

~

lily hyacinth winifred pearl
is a very   very pretty girl

but   she has a tiny flaw   you see
that she once showed to little me

it's one silly simple fact
about how sometimes she might act

if lily does not get her way
& this is something I can say

with authority on the matter
because I watched her mouth get fatter

fatter and fatter   about to explode
and what came out when it did...oh no!

~

snarling rats and slithering snakes
came flying out   for goodness sake

stinging ants crawled up the walls
bats flew about with ugly claws

the room filled up with dark and dread
i had to quickly hide my head

lily hyacinth winifred pearl
is a very very pretty girl

but if this is lily's tantrum day
i suggest   you run away!

crazy rain

drip drop drizzle
nana's in a tizzle

she wants to hang the sheets to dry
but rain is pouring from the sky

hip hip hop
bunny's in a slop

his ears are wet   his food is too
his hay is brown   his nose is blue

jack e flew the coop
he's dancing on the stoop

he's not indoors where boys belong
when clouds are dripping all day long

his mother makes a shout
you must not be out!

i must be out! sweet jack e quipped
& down the street sweet jack e skipped

oopee doopie doo
doo wop doolittle too

how many drops can a rain cloud drop
how many thunders can it roll
how many strikes of lightening light
    does it take to light the night
how many times must a mother say
i don't know   please go and play

when the dreary dribbly drops
dripping from the wet rooftops
have stolen all the sunny sun
how does a child have any fun

you must make do with tents and frizzles
paint your face to get through the drizzles

write a sunny story play
to make the crazy rain go 'way

be king of the mountain on top of your bunk
build a cool robot out of old junk

unload the closet   wear all your clothes
put your shoes on your head
put your socks on your nose

fold some paper and build a plane
build another   do it again

turn on the fan and let it blow
see how far these planes will go

slither and slather in a bathtub lather
bubble your trouble down the drain

never fear   there is plenty dear
to do in a crazy rain

how to make mud pie

when the sky   wipes its eyes
—dim thunder   rumbling

run outside

wave like squawking birds
converge   on a makeshift lake

rainwater running to greet you
wade in

barefoot   flex your toes
           stretch their necks

           stand   knee deep
           in rainwater

    ~

a few fat drops shower you
cold wet clothes—cling

stomp
splash

sing in the street
—rain dance
—glee club

goose bumps

    ~

squat   squish mud
between your toes
shovel up a clump of

—oozing earth

fling it
at the first   (unsuspecting)
friend

—splat—a flinched face

—splat—an arched back

—splat—a burst of laughter

i got you!

~

now you are merciless:
warriors   taking aim

duck
dive

slip
slide

run

from each other
like you   might really
die

in seconds
    an hour passes

    ~

your breath comes fast
full of fun & covered
in mud pie

    ~

lie down in the long   green
grass   in the gutter
bent   under
this sudden stream

    let fresh water
—wash   you clean

riddle

i can be found on rainy days
with a wet and shiny face

in the spot little mara plays
in her very favorite place

a squishy squashy mess am i
when i am mixed with muddy pie

if barefoot mara jumps in me
i become a droplet sea

i seem to disappear in air
i have not gone   i still am there!

(a puddle)

riddle ii

three   round rosy rings
where the high trapezes swing

elephants kneel on wrinkled knees
children squeal   happy & pleased

striped tent   red and white
glowing fiber-optic light

jump and swirl with loud delight
lions roar—it's popcorn night!

(circus)

words gone wild

rum-chuttle rum chuttle rum-chuttle rum
crow clack clatter   snap dragon fun

pop sizzle rattle drag a chair across the floor
don't know about you but i can do more

chimmi-chimmi changa   cock-a-doodle-do
mouse in the corner what's a girl to do

hold your breath   count to ten
hop-scotch puddle jump do it again

zip slap whack click
light a red match blow it out real quick

looked in the closet and under the bed
between my toes and over my head

jingle jingle jangle   queen of kung fu
it's all over now i lost my left shoe

snicky snicky juju box
bright red hair on a goldie locks

half-moon   honey moon
oops i think i spoke too soon

a duck's cluck   a stinky truck
hold on a minute i think i'm stuck

cotton candy   english peas
it ain't easy making rhymes like these

jitterbug   cut-a-rug
snuggle up love in a great big hug

hip-hop dance   take a chance
long legged spider with ants in his pants

billy goats wearing petticoats
farmer in a straw hat sewing some oats

upstairs brown bears hula-hoops and cradles
mama kissing daddy   hot soup with ladles

hot stuff in a huff hoot owls too
words gone wild it's a hulabaloo!

wild cats

deep in the jungle lives
a big old cat whose name is
panther billy mack   his

hair is black   his eyes are green
baddest cat you've ever seen

tip tap twist shout
saturday night's for stepping out

~

lep the leopard really loves the blues
both cats wear their dancing shoes

tiger ups some fancy shades
best striped suit   some roller blades

lep slicks back his spotted hair
these three cats don't have a care

~

jazzy cats who really love to move
cats who can scat some groovy jazz tunes too

bop diddly doo wop ba ba ba hey
underneath the gaze of the milky way
dance all night   sleep all day

where the goblins go

way down deep where the willawogs grow
where the creatures creep and the goblins go

where wigglies and worms uproot the soil
where headless fish make stink and spoil

a wild witch sits in a rocking chair
a wicked wind in her wiry hair

her crooked hands and gnarly feet
tap to the music of an eerie beat

round and round in a circle dance
chicketts and drummons hop and prance

their scarlet bellies and yellow claws
click and bounce as they clap their paws

orange feathers and lime green beaks
sniff the air, say SOMETHING REEKS!

tip-toe through the hazy blue
—careful that the willawog doesn't catch you!

don't pet the puppy
unless you want to take him home

puppy's breath has special smells
puppy's breath casts magic spells

here's a warning from the start
puppy's breath will steal your heart

there's no doubt his big brown eyes
tell   *i'll be no trouble*—lies

he'll roll over   tummy up
begging you to pick him up

his puppy tail will wiggle
his lick will make you giggle

if you get a little whiff
if you get a teensy sniff

of that puppy's magic smell
—you're caught in the puppy spell

now you have to take him home
he'll be yours—   your very own

baby's song

baby rides
in mother's car
home from market
it's not far

baby waits
at mailbox stop
into its mouth
lets letters drop

baby hears
a windy chime
overhead
a cessna whine

seed pod rattles
across concrete
oak leaves fall
—a sienna sheet

dandelions   &
red buds bloom
toad hip-hopping on
a huge mushroom

soon   a treat for
baby's eyes
sandhill cranes
will vee the sky

~

wild march hair
miss spring does grow
with bluebonnet ribbons
& honey bee bows

to wit to twit
tap tap to wee
she sings this ditty
chick chick chickadee

her jumping dandy
jiggery-jig
in magenta skirts
makes a sound so big

her rumbling tumbling
whirling twirl
makes brand new babies
for a brand new world

the longest shadow

night wondering

what's going on in the houses 'round the town
what goes on when the sun goes down

mama's in her pj's standing at the sink
rollers in her hair—gets a good night drink

daddy's in his easy chair leaning back to think
scratch behind the dog's ear—falling off to sleep

sister's in the bathroom—bubbles in the tub
scrubbing up her toenails—rub-a-dub-dub

brother's in the bedroom jumping on the bed
giggling when mama screams *gonna hit your head*

baby's in her cradle sucking on her thumb
dreaming about the lullabies nana hums

nana's in the attic taking out her teeth—
she'll saw enough logs to last a whole week

kitty wants a slurp of milk—MEOW, MEOW, MEOW
wouldn't she be happy if she had her own cow

crickets in the carpet   sing a nighttime song
everybody stretches and sighs a big yawn

mama hugs the children—pats the baby's back
daddy raids the kitchen for a late-night snack

nana shuts the attic door—blows the kids a kiss
catch them in the air—be careful not to miss

nana's things

potpourri piled in crystal vases
smells like roses in my noses

a hot hot oven bakes chocolate chips
my lips lick the messy bits

barefoot chasing chickety-chicks
run in the yard   lickety-splits

ice cubes   sugar cubes
click in a glass

tea sips   wiggly hips
     —spin real fast

dance in the kitchen
wear a silly hat

popcorn in a skillet
makes nana so fat

dishes in the sink
games that make you think

tunes on the turntable
puzzle on the kitchen table

froggy goggles dive in the swimming pool
win a game of bocce ball   act real cool

chase the chihuahua round and round
you can't catch that wily hound

pitch a tent   put a stake in the ground
listen to the nighttime creature sounds:

dry wood crackling on a yellow fire
hoot owl hooting as he flies nearby-er

racoon's scoot
opossum's snoot

toads that sing
chimes that ring

when you love someone

you like the way they smell
—but   not always

when you love someone
you like the things they do

—but   not always

when you love someone
you want to see their face
and you can't wait for them

to come home

when you love someone
you like the way they dress

even when they put their
shirt on backwards   or
wear their pink tutu
with lime green and turquoise

striped socks

when you love someone
you love the things they love

even when they want
to watch the same movie
eleven times

you watch it with them

when you love someone
you want to share everything
with them—well   maybe not

everything

when you love someone
you hurt when they hurt
and when they're sick

you bring them breakfast in bed

when you love someone
& they feel happy
you feel happy   too

& when they feel sad
—you feel sad

sometimes   when two people
are very sad   it makes everything
around them feel all droopy and blue

even the room and the rooster and the moon

when you love someone
and they lose their happy
you help them find it

even if it takes all day

even if it takes all night

when you love someone
holding their hand
makes your heart feel
all warm and fuzzy

& you want
to take them
with you

everywhere

when you feel really scared
    or grumpy

you want to cuddle up next to them

but most of all
when it is time for bed
you want someone you love

to hold your sleepy head

soon i must go to bed

but   not before the sun
sinks beneath the purple skirted earth

not until he yawns   below
the long blue line   dividing day
     —from night

not until his hundred hands
hold   their golden fingers

high above his fiery head

not until then must i go to bed

~

soon i must go to bed

but   not before the mud hen
roosts by the dark green pond

not until she hang-glides through the
thin pink skin of twilight

not until her soft brown wing
hides her curled duck head

not until then must i go to bed

~

soon i must go to bed

but   not before the lullaby
floats   from the open throat
of the croaking toad

not before his staccato song
calls the mossy shadows
from the hollow log

not before he blinks
—round amber eyes
on his amphibious head

not until then must i go to bed

~

soon i must go to bed

but   not before the vanilla moon
weaves her warp and waft

not before her gossamer thread has
veiled the dark trees and lit the pasture grass

not before the pixie's bath
in her shimmering white pools

not until then must i go to bed

~

soon i must go to bed

but   not before the evening breeze
teases the four-o-clock bloom

makes her bring her magenta face
out from her secret hiding place

not before the longest shadow
becomes a giant striding

across her glistening breast

not until she holds
her constant nighttime breath

not until then must i go to bed

clouds at sunset

soft pink seashell floating in the sky
dark red snapper swimming closely by

light blue feathers sweeping up the mess
lazy gray crocodile: stretch   yawn   rest

white barking poodle chasing after ball
golden stalks of wheat grow twelve feet tall

lavender ribbon kissed with a pearl
whippoorwill sings sweet dreams to the world

About the Author

D. Ellis Phelps' poems, essays, and visual art have appeared widely online and in print. As an educator, she has taught fine arts in various venues with students of all ages for decades, & she currently facilitates The Art of Writing Workshop Series for the Patrick Heath Public Library in Boerne, Texas, among other venues.

In addition to having edited more than a dozen anthologies, she is the author of two books of poetry: *what she holds* (Moon Shadow Sanctuary Press, 2020) & *what holds her* (Main Street Rag, 2019) & of the novel, *Making Room for George* (MSSP, 2016). On her blog, *Formidable Woman Sanctuary,* she writes about spiritual and emotional healing and the writing life, among other topics, while also publishing the work of other writers and artists.

She is the founding and managing editor of Moon Shadow Sanctuary Press and of *fws: international journal of literature & art.*